A PICTURE BOOK

THE THAMES

BY THEO BERGSTROM

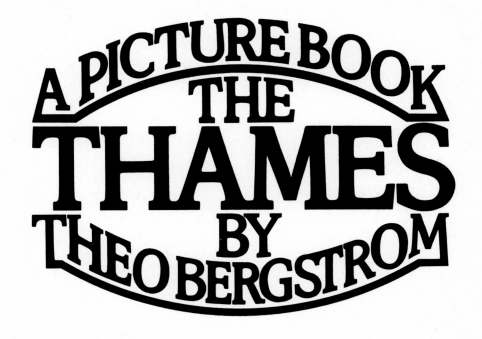

A PICTURE BOOK
THE
THAMES
BY
THEO BERGSTROM

Bergström + Boyle Books, London

Produced and published by Bergström + Boyle Books Limited
22 Maddox Street, London W1R 9PG

Photographs   © Theo Bergström 1975
Text   © Michael Black 1975

Map design: Tamasin Cole
Cover lettering: David Quay
Art bromides: John Couzins

Printed in Great Britain by Butler & Tanner Ltd
The Selwood Printing Works, Frome, Somerset

Bound by J. M. Dent & Sons Ltd, The Aldine Press,
Dunhams Lane, Letchworth, Herts.

ISBN 0 903767 04 X

These photographs were taken on the river in early summer from Thames Head down to Southend.

2

4

8

11

12

15

16

18

19

24

29

30

31

34

44

62

THEY SAY that the letters TH can be seen carved in the trunk of the grey ash-tree in Trewsbury Mead, marking the spot called Thames Head. Do not expect a bold, clear inscription, the bark has covered the cut, but if you let your eye wander for a while you will see TH carved several times; and if you stay quietly, as I did, in the first light of a May morning, maybe the loose stones at the foot of the tree will form into the well-head that served the Romans from the nearby camp. There's no water now, which makes the spot the more magical, only the shallowest of green valleys slopes away to the south, and overall there's a stillness, a grandeur about this spot, it feels like the very heart of England. Go down that gentle green valley, cross the Fosse Way and soon, your feet wet, you will see the first of the giant water-docks and suddenly a sparkling carpet of white and gold crowfoot; just about there, is a spring of bright clean water that wells up from the ground, collects together watercress and tasselled weeds and hurries away to the first village as a busy river should.

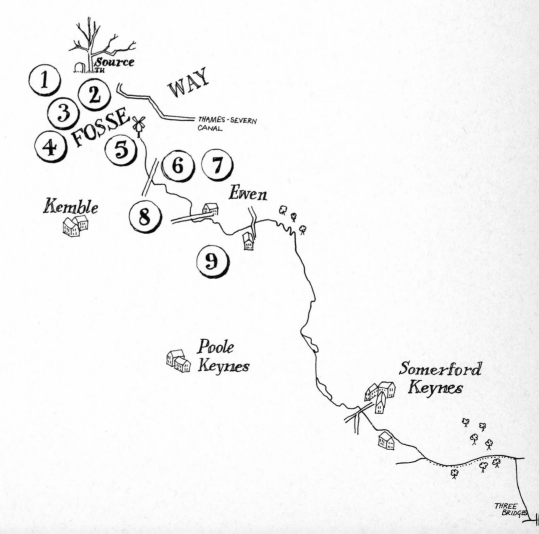

As the little river Thames makes its way through this upper region it has a distinctive air of purpose, not fast nor slow, but busy, collecting together the tributaries, adding to itself and dividing. The land hereabouts is, in the main, Keynes country – Poole Keynes, Ashton Keynes and Somerford – taking their names from Sir John who held the land under Richard II. There are other local names with ancient river associations, Kemble, some think, being the modern spelling of Cumulos, the Celtic god, and Ewen is from the Old English *aewielm* – the spring, source of a river.

It is not possible to put a boat on the water yet, it's too shallow, though the Swill Brook joining near Ashton Keynes, makes quite a difference; it's noticeable how the river gradually grows in stature, willows start to line the banks and the banks themselves are better defined, there are deeper pools of water at the bends and soon the River is wide enough for swans to land.

The swans on this upper Thames are wilder, they raise their heads immediately a traveller comes into view, watch every movement and if approached fly away; it's noticeable too that the coot and moorhen above Lechlade fly faster, getting up off the water cleanly, flying higher and further out of harm's way.

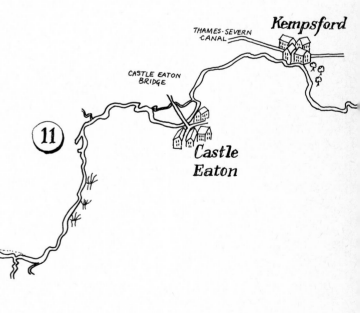

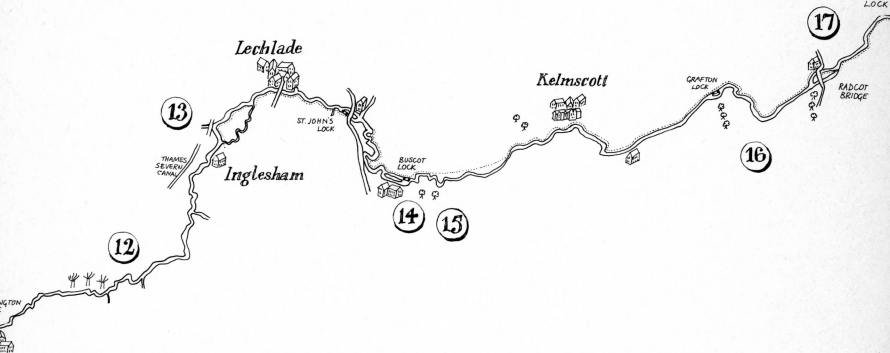

At Cricklade the old Thames-Severn Canal comes close to the River again. It had gone off on its own, way back near Thames Head, having been fed by a considerable pumping station, and it comes in from the left now quite close, running its last few miles on a near parallel course until the last lock at Inglesham Roundhouse.

This beautiful house, with its lush weeping willows and thick rushes, has lost all its former glory and now remains but a pretty monument to a grand idea that never succeeded. In 1633 the first mention occurs in records of a splendid notion 'ffor the Contryving of Navigation betweene the Ryvers of the Thames and Seaverne' (Thacker Volume II p32), and thirty-five years later in the Lord's Journals for 1688 is mention of 'a draft Act for making an inland passage', and in the Gentleman's Magazine of 19th November 1780 we read that 'a boat . . . passed laden for the first time to St. John's Bridge, below Lechlade, in the presence of great numbers, who answered a salute of twelve pieces of cannon from Buscott Park by loud Huzzas'. There was a dinner, bell-ringing, a bonfire, and a ball. But by 1816 the City Surveyors criticized the decayed state of the canal and by 1881 it was proposed to close it – the tolls that year amounting to £3 6s. 10d. Then in 1883 the Great Western Railway bought the canal, promising to push their new railway line through from Lechlade to Bristol (which they still haven't done!). In 1889 one canal boat passed through. And in 1920 patient Fred Thacker reports sadly of an infrequent dredger disturbing the peace of the wolfish pike . . .

It is at Inglesham that the River changes again. There is a sudden widening on the turn where water flows in from the Coln, and this widening gives long views of dappled water and rippling silver light that please the eye. The River begins to move with a grand air, with a tread measured by restraining weirs and locks. In these days of leisure and pleasure it is good to remember that the establishment of locks and weirs was a very serious matter and the cause of a long and bitter struggle between the three groups with a vested interest in the River.

There were the riparian owners and their tenants of mills and fishfarms who made easy money out of the water power and deeper pools that weirs provided. There were the bargefolk and merchants who wanted clear navigation and deep water. And there were all those who lived beside the River who were frightened of the floods caused by the weirs and whose livelihood largely depended on fishing. Weirs were the only form of control over the water until the 1660's when the first locks were built. As early as 1066 there is a Royal Proclamation about these weirs, showing support for the bargemen: 'if mills, fisheries, are constructed to the rivers' hindrance, let these works be destroyed, the Waters repaired.' This refers to the four Royal Rivers – the Thames, the Severn, the Trent and the Yorkshire Ouse. Clearly some way had to be devised to hold up sufficient water for the passage of boats. The fishermen, the millers and the bargemen all wanted the use of the River, preferably without payment, and the River was vital – it was the country's highway.

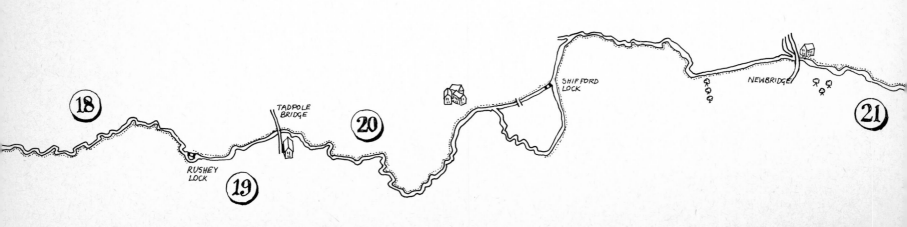

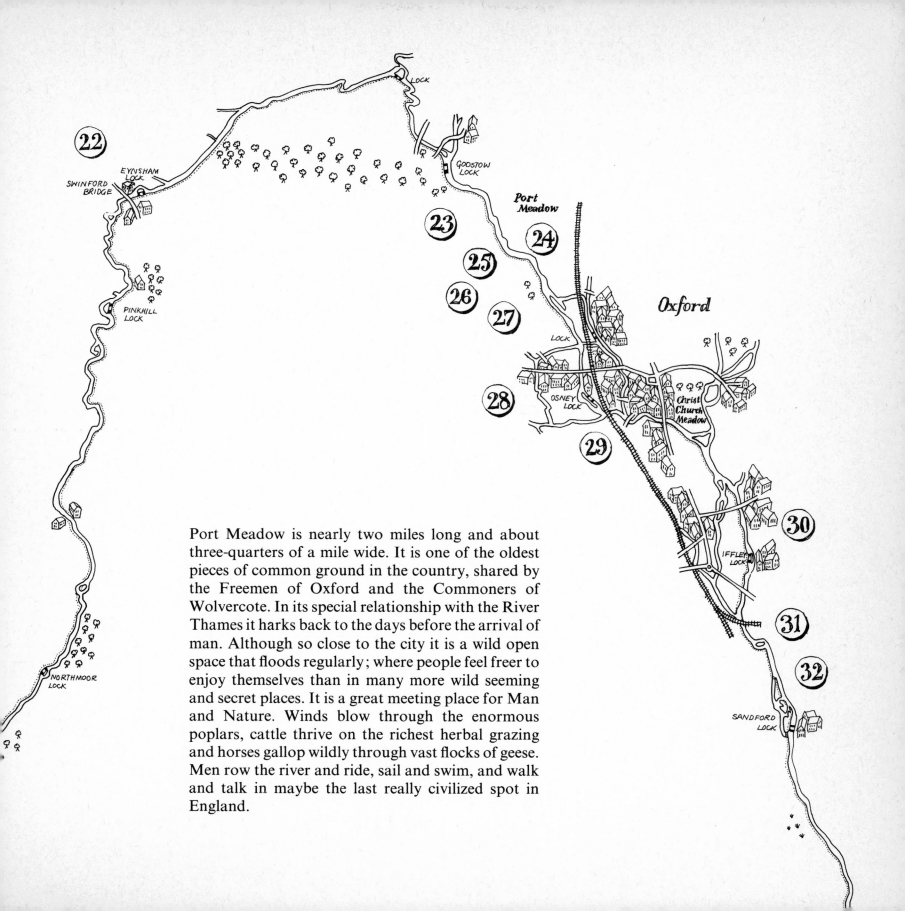

Port Meadow is nearly two miles long and about three-quarters of a mile wide. It is one of the oldest pieces of common ground in the country, shared by the Freemen of Oxford and the Commoners of Wolvercote. In its special relationship with the River Thames it harks back to the days before the arrival of man. Although so close to the city it is a wild open space that floods regularly; where people feel freer to enjoy themselves than in many more wild seeming and secret places. It is a great meeting place for Man and Nature. Winds blow through the enormous poplars, cattle thrive on the richest herbal grazing and horses gallop wildly through vast flocks of geese. Men row the river and ride, sail and swim, and walk and talk in maybe the last really civilized spot in England.

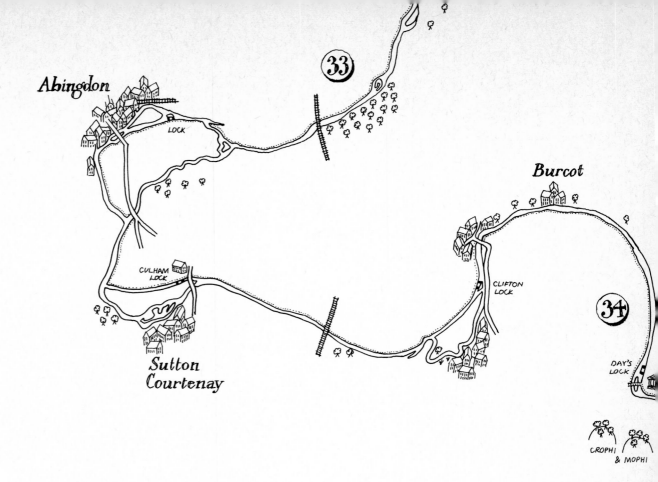

Richard I's second charter reads: 'Know ye all that we, for the health of our soul, our fathers soul, and all our ancestors souls, and also for the Common Weal of our city of London, and of all our realm, have granted and steadfastly commanded that all weirs that are in the Thames be removed.' It seemed to take an eternity for these three parties to understand that their interests interlocked, watermills needed a head of water for power, the millcuts that held this harboured fine fat fish, and these deep water stretches between weirs made for greater ease of navigation. These separate needs and benefits began to be coordinated only about 1600 with the formation of the first Thames Commission, the Oxford-Burcott, which, being vested with certain local powers, managed to build a few proper locks. Abingdon, Reading and Windsor also acquired local jurisdiction over the River. The three earliest Thames 'turnpikes' were Iffley, Sandford and Swift Ditch in 1660 – somewhat behind the times since Exeter Canal had a lock in 1573 and locks had been used in Lombardy since the turn of the fifteenth century.

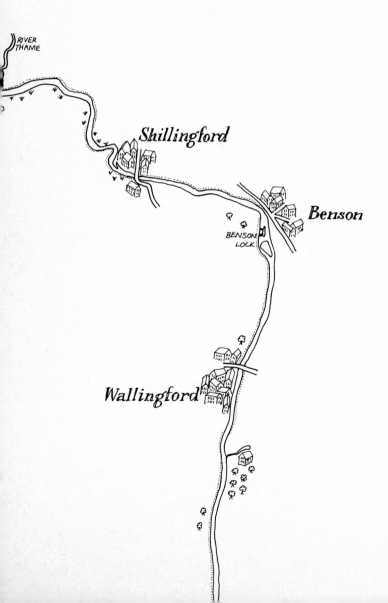

Now the River is better organized, most locks are electrically operated, only a few paddle and rymer weirs are left, constant dredging goes on from barges and bank, men in lonely twos and threes spend years scooping up the mud and building up the banks. The cuts are clean, the mills for the most part gone, often destroyed by fire, and the fishermen arrive at four o'clock on a Sunday morning in charabancs from Birmingham.

Between Oxford and Henley the River describes a great loop. We leave that low gravel bank which lies protected between the Isis and the Cherwell, and soon see Sinodun, Wittenham Clumps – or Crophi and Mophi if you prefer it – the ancient camp and burial ground overlooking the Neolithic and Bronze Age dwellings that covered the opposite bank and were later taken over by the Romans as an important centre. Shillingford and Wallingford are both old local crossing places but the earliest and busiest must have been down at Streatley where that ancient way the Icknield comes down for a moment from the hills.

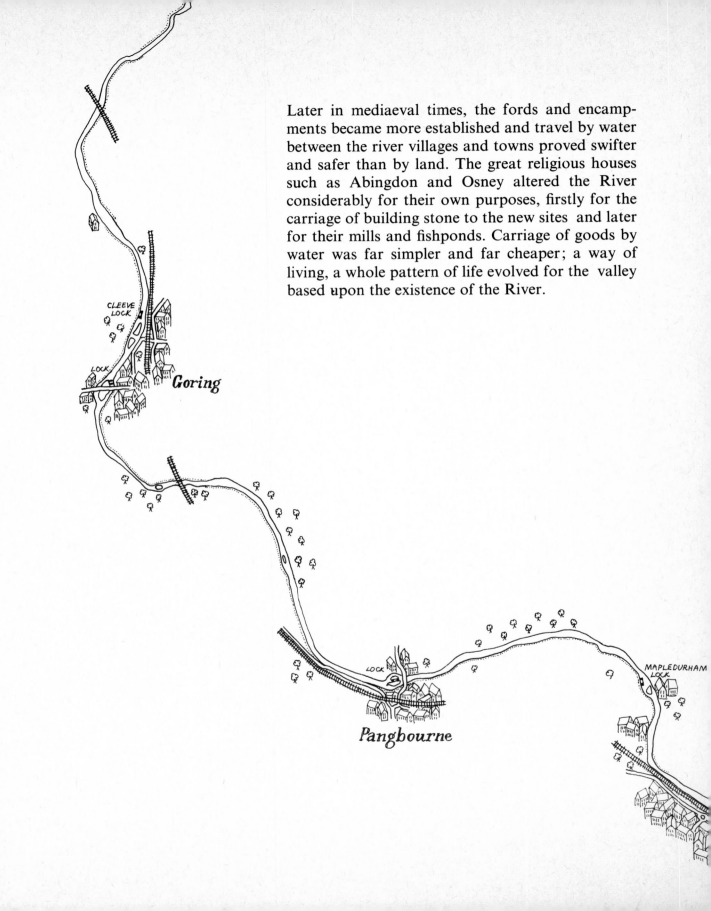

Later in mediaeval times, the fords and encampments became more established and travel by water between the river villages and towns proved swifter and safer than by land. The great religious houses such as Abingdon and Osney altered the River considerably for their own purposes, firstly for the carriage of building stone to the new sites and later for their mills and fishponds. Carriage of goods by water was far simpler and far cheaper; a way of living, a whole pattern of life evolved for the valley based upon the existence of the River.

CLEEVE
LOCK

LOCK

Goring

LOCK

MAPLEDURHAM
LOCK

Pangbourne

Henley has a special place not just in the hearts of the rowing fraternity and their camp followers, but of all who know the Thames. Henley alone has not turned its back on the River. The houses go down to meet the water and the boats are moored on the pavements. It has garlanded the River with a beautiful bridge, decorated the bridge with carved heads of Isis and Tamesis and crowned the great rowing reach with the Temple and the first Lombardy poplars planted in England. The River itself acknowledges this homage with a serious air, assumes a grander manner and, shouldering a thick mantle of great trees that crowd the steep banks and colour the water the darkest green, looks toward Royal Windsor and the City of London.

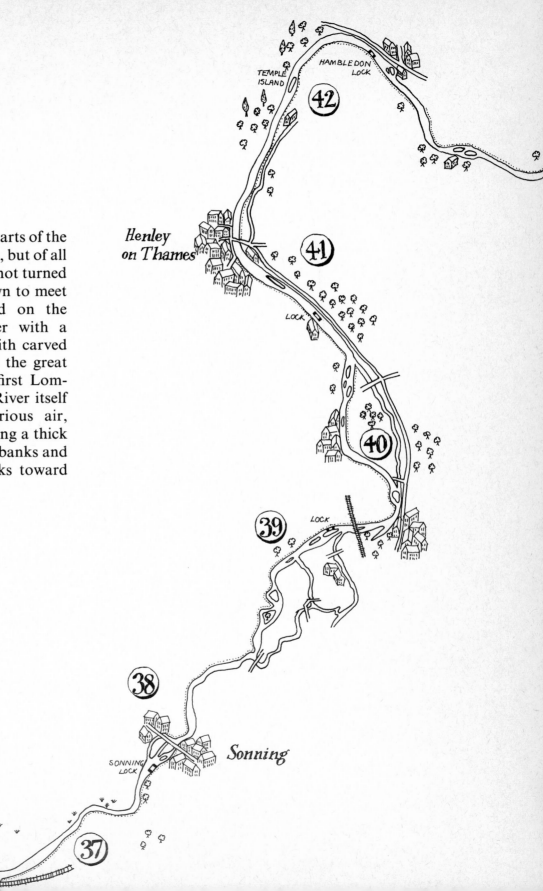

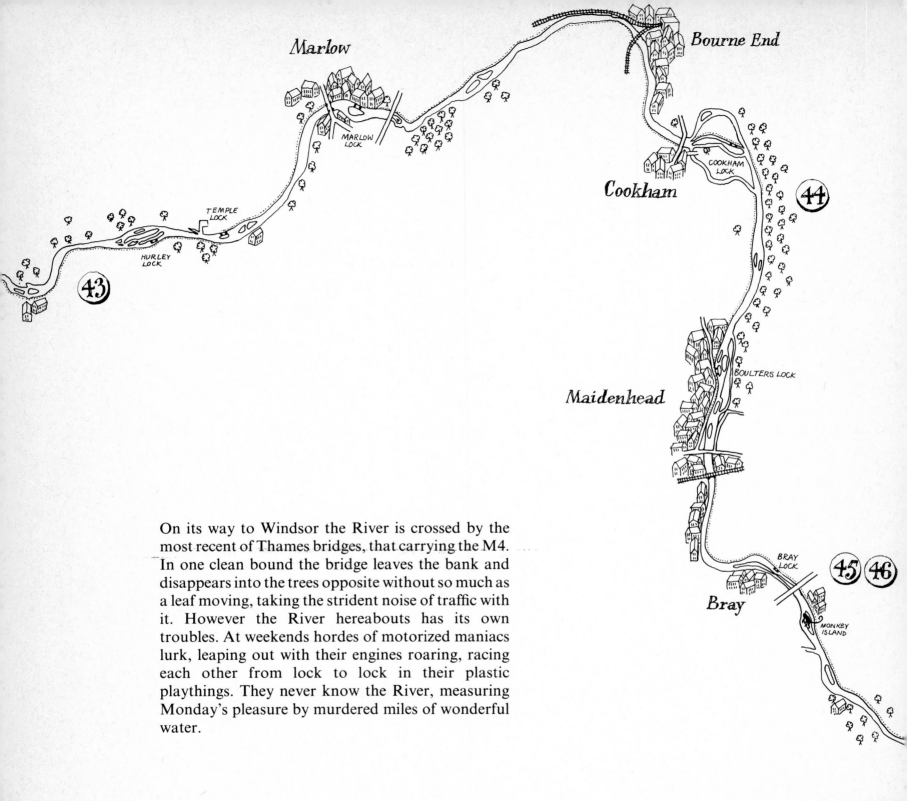

On its way to Windsor the River is crossed by the most recent of Thames bridges, that carrying the M4. In one clean bound the bridge leaves the bank and disappears into the trees opposite without so much as a leaf moving, taking the strident noise of traffic with it. However the River hereabouts has its own troubles. At weekends hordes of motorized maniacs lurk, leaping out with their engines roaring, racing each other from lock to lock in their plastic playthings. They never know the River, measuring Monday's pleasure by murdered miles of wonderful water.

But if you row a proper boat, have no fear of the mere passers-by, be wary of their wash, be patient, they soon disappear, and quiet returns. There are beautiful boating reaches here, and several old established clubs. On these stretches there were once so many boats out in summer that the locks and rollers jammed with gay laughing river-lovers, and the occasional sibilant steam launch. Boat builders' yards still abound, the material they use now is mainly fibreglass but they often bear the original name, names famous up to Oxford and down to London – the Bossoms, the Bassons and the Beasleys, Harris and Timm's, Salters and Collins – names that have been on the River for hundreds of years. The Beasleys came down from Cumberland to be watermen at Oxford in the early fourteenth century and they are still here, many within a mile of the River. These families are as old in their trade as the bargemen and the London Watermen, right through the centuries they have been ferrymen, millers, boat-builders, lock-keepers and fishermen.

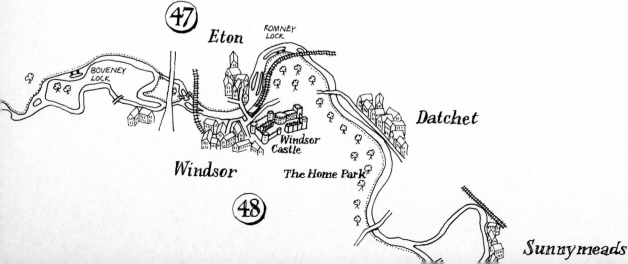

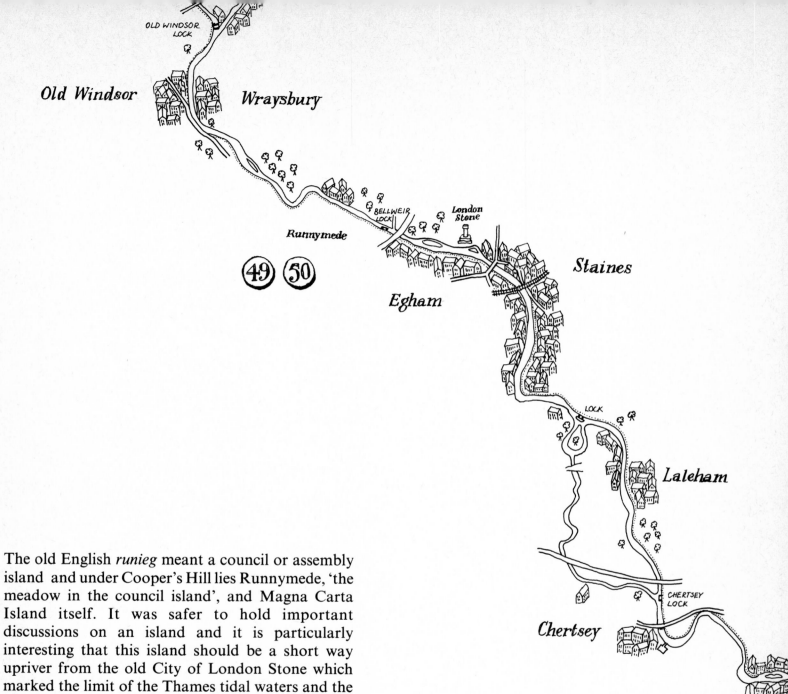

The old English *runieg* meant a council or assembly island and under Cooper's Hill lies Runnymede, 'the meadow in the council island', and Magna Carta Island itself. It was safer to hold important discussions on an island and it is particularly interesting that this island should be a short way upriver from the old City of London Stone which marked the limit of the Thames tidal waters and the western boundary of the City's power over the Thames. The Thames Conservancy, incorporated in 1857, extended their jurisdiction eastward from the Stone to Teddington in 1909. The Stone also marks the county boundaries of Buckinghamshire, Surrey and Middlesex.

It is in the reaches between Kingston and the last Thames lock at Teddington that you suddenly get a whiff of the sea and the great maritime world beyond the Port of London. Coasters come up this far to trade and you may be passed by the Port of London police launch, keeping an eye on large barges and tugs. The dredger sitting in the middle of the River is there on business.

Teddington or Tudintun in the year 969 was the Tun of Tuda's people, spelt variously Tead or Tod. Some people interpret the name to mean 'tide-end-town' but this is unlikely for the tides used to rise as high as Staines and as late as March 1909 there was a tide high enough to carry a barge up through the lock without the gates being operated.

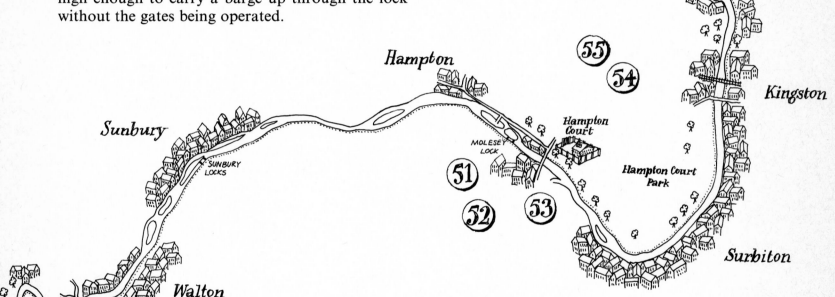

He who travels in a frail craft on the stripling Thames from Shrewsbury Mead and on to the Isis at Oxford, and is carried by the sweet Thames that runs through the heart of England, meets the now fully tidal river at Teddington with a shock. The River, having helped fisherman and farmer, having tolerated generations of young rowing men and even the language of bargees, and allowed itself to be harnessed and directed, now suddenly at Teddington asserts its power and becomes the London River.

London River is a different river. As you come out of Teddington Lock at any time between high tides, the smell changes. The sweet country scents of field and riverside trees are overwhelmed by the smell of London River: not offensive nowadays, simply the pungency of the bare river mud. Soon the banks have sharper, more eroded edges, the mud looks harder, and is worked into strange shapes polished by the endless movement of the water. On the mud rest the deposits of each tide, all sorts of flotsam and jetsam at many different heights. The reeds that grow on top are half dirty half clean and every tree lining the bank shows you where the water has been. The River now becomes very brisk, both men and boats must obey the rules. That tiny stream that dallied through duckweed and watercress in the hills now spins great barges round twice a day by the nose. In a boat you may run down with the tide in the centre, carried swiftly and strongly to sea; but if you go against the tide you must skulk along the bank using every stretch of slack water you can find. You pass a few fully-laden lighters waiting to unload and a few empty ones moored to wharves, waiting to be towed downstream. Even the rowing boats on the London

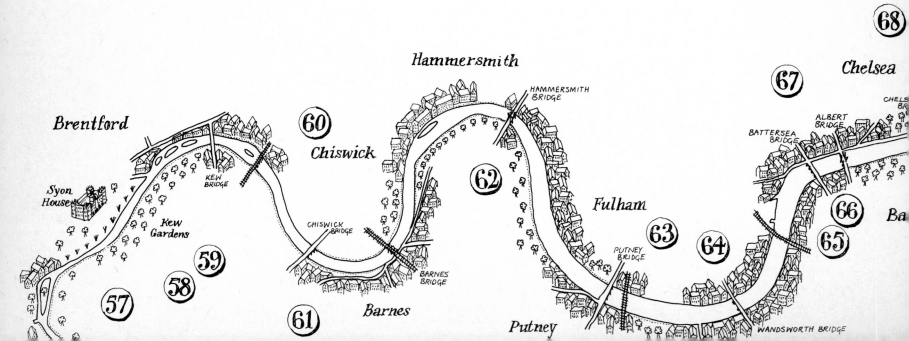

River are a different shape: heavier, broader, but still beautifully built and elegant. They are safer for these reaches than an Upper Thames skiff would be: tugs towing lighters have no time to watch their wash. And as the River passes under bridges, fast-flowing water piles up against the piers, curling into whirlpools round the pillars, then forming a brooding swell of light and shadow. Driftwood, large and small, glides and dances by the buoys, tipped by the tide. Past palaces, power houses and Parliament the London River, taking the last bridges in one rush, enters the great Pool of London.

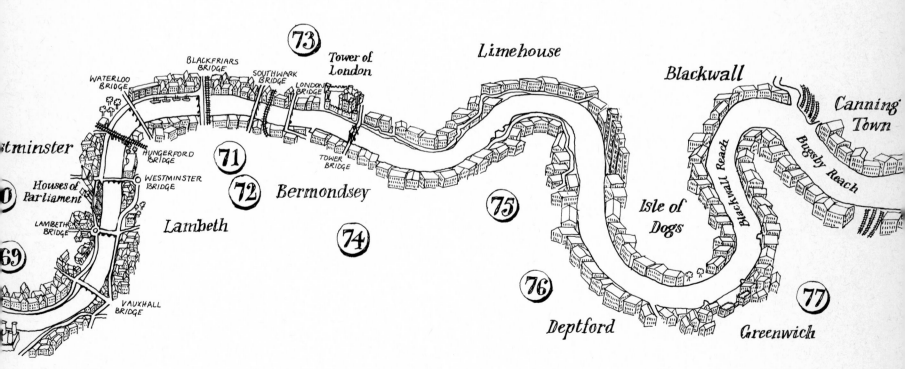

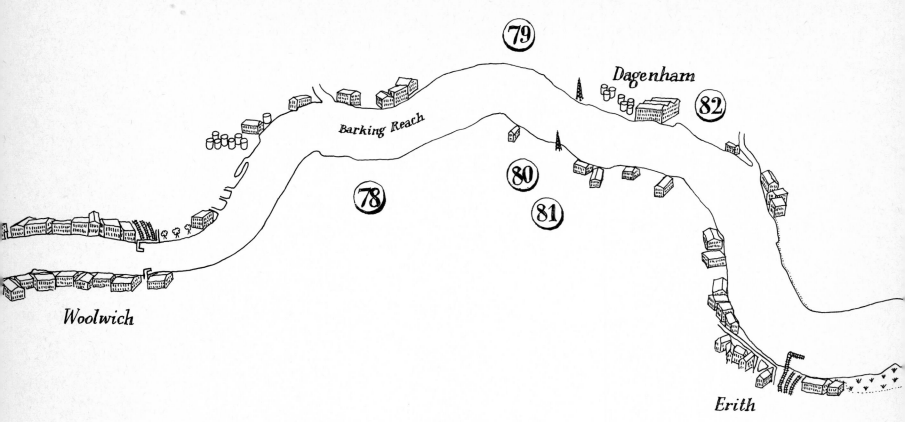

As we leave Greenwich to travel down the last few reaches to Gravesend, through Blackwall and Bugsby, Barking and Fiddlers, the River itself is fast disappearing – it is still the Thames but Greenwich was the last building that respected its dignity and we now pass through miles of industrial squalor. We also pass the greatest docks in the world, the Royal Docks of Victoria, Albert and George V. All this land on each bank down to Woolwich and Shooter's Hill was once part of that garden of London that stretched away to the east and the estuary. A rich soil that could grow wondrous crops existed here, Celia Fiennes in about 1700 described it as a land clothed with trees, grass and flowers, gardens and orchards, with all sorts of herbage and tillage.

Now all that can be seen is an occasional huddle of allotments between sprawling concrete buildings and belching chimneys; further down from Woolwich vast undeveloped marshes seethe with smoking refuse tips. Originally the River and the sea at high tide sprawled out across a much wider area, the River Lea, Barking Creek and Dartford Creek added their sluggish waters, and it took many hundred years of patient thought and constant toil to make the waterway safe and to wrest that rich agricultural land from the sea. Next we arrive at Tilbury, its docks and tidal basin nowadays more important than all the Pool of London, handling vast quantities of merchandise in containers. While across the River on a slight hill there still exists the Roman village of Vagniacae, newly excavated.

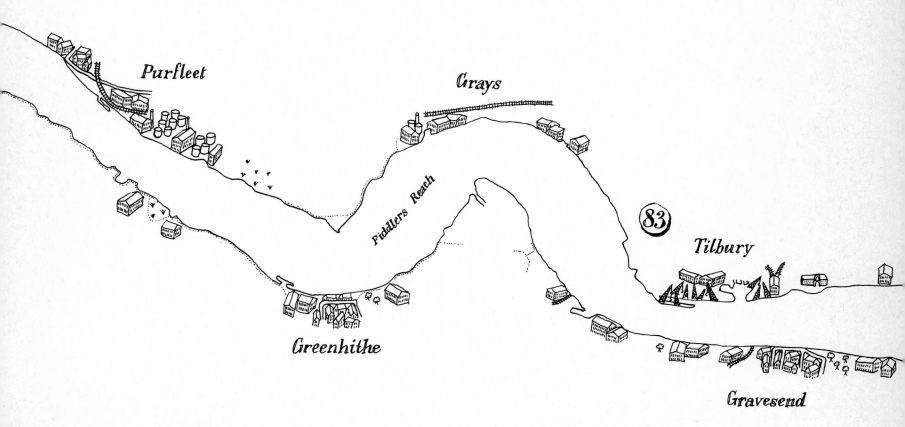

Gravesend – Gravesham in the Doomsday Book – may mean at the 'end of the grove'. In many ways it marks the last stretch of the River; beyond Gravesend marshes reach out to the sea, it is the first and last town that serves the Thames, the place where the sea and river pilots hand over their charges. With Tilbury it forms a splendid gateway to the country – here are the riverside defences against the marauding Dutch and French, and this farthest point is where Queen Elizabeth defied the Armada of Spain.

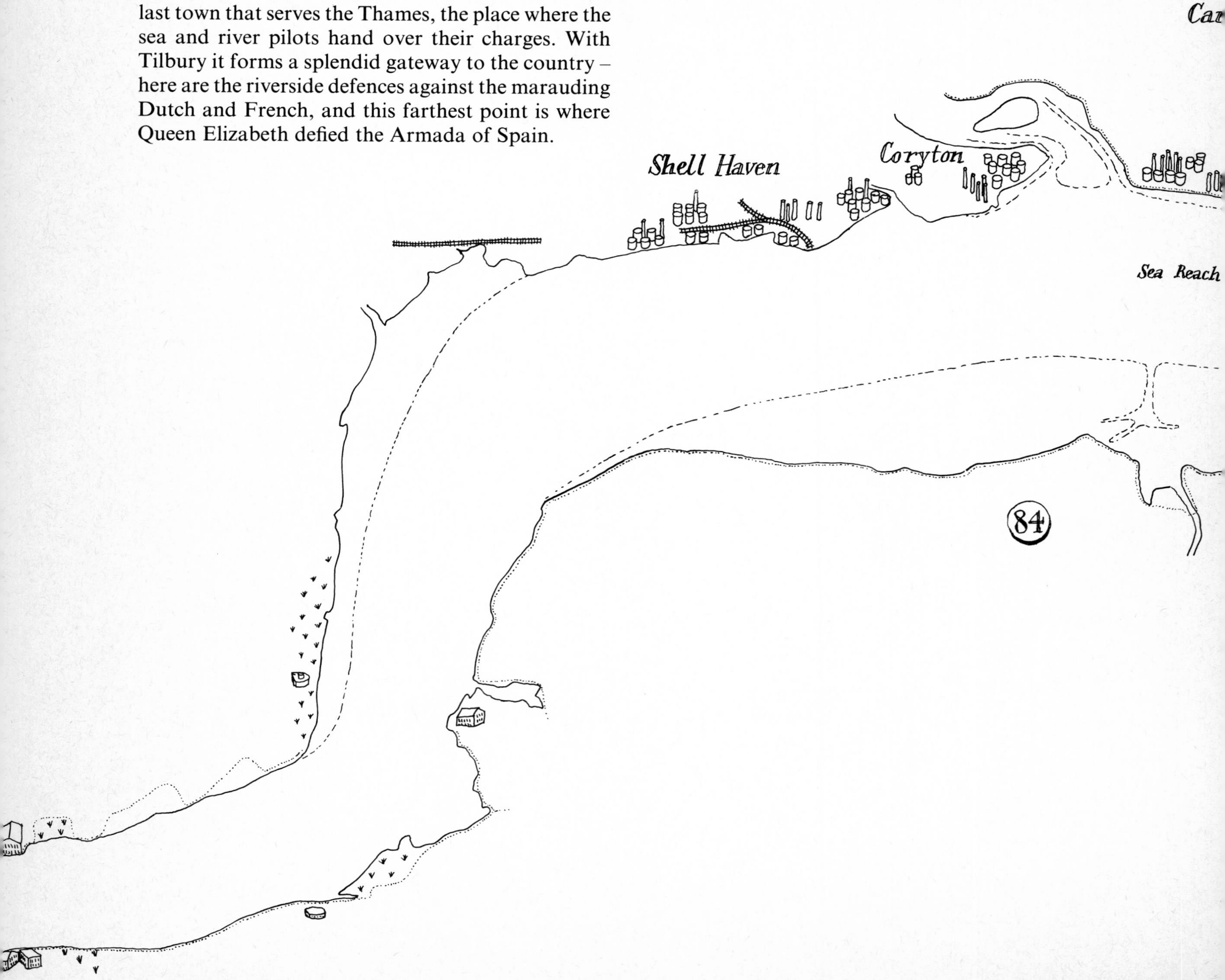

Car

Coryton

Shell Haven

Sea Reach

84

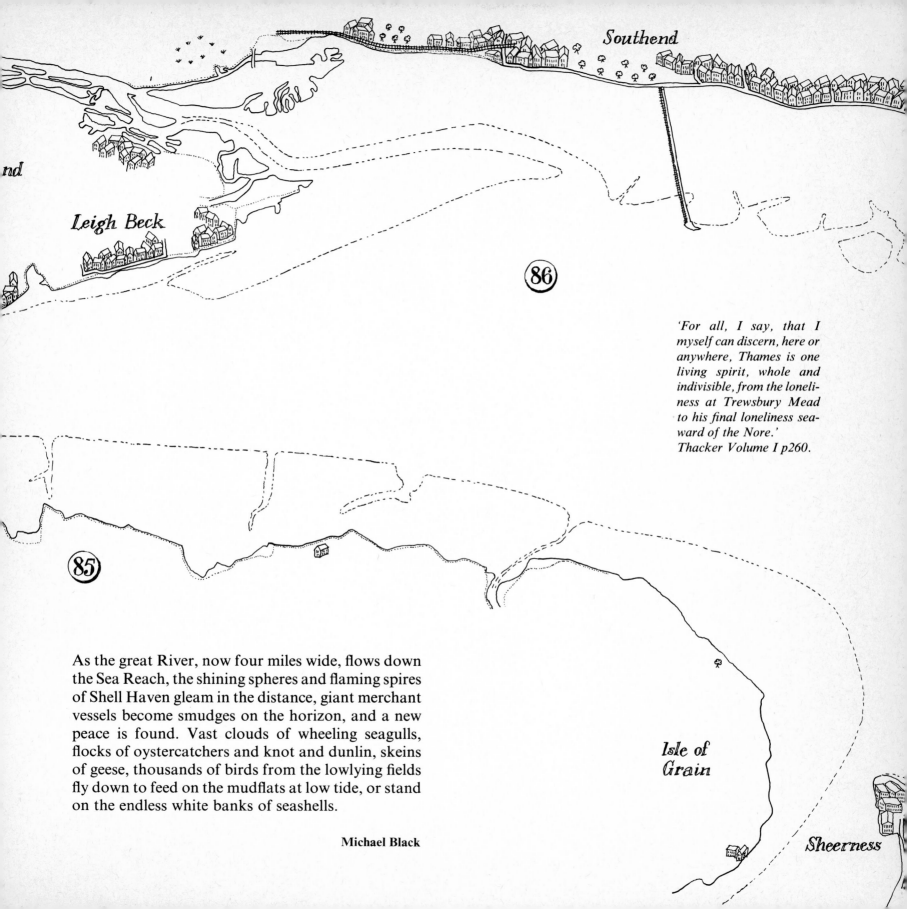

nd

Southend

Leigh Beck

86

85

'For all, I say, that I myself can discern, here or anywhere, Thames is one living spirit, whole and indivisible, from the loneliness at Trewsbury Mead to his final loneliness seaward of the Nore.'
Thacker Volume I p260.

As the great River, now four miles wide, flows down the Sea Reach, the shining spheres and flaming spires of Shell Haven gleam in the distance, giant merchant vessels become smudges on the horizon, and a new peace is found. Vast clouds of wheeling seagulls, flocks of oystercatchers and knot and dunlin, skeins of geese, thousands of birds from the lowlying fields fly down to feed on the mudflats at low tide, or stand on the endless white banks of seashells.

Michael Black

Isle of Grain

Sheerness

Bibliography

Nicholson's Guide to the Thames. 1969.

Fred S. Thacker: The Thames Highway, 2 vols, 1914.
            Reprinted 1968.

Fred S. Thacker: The Stripling Thames. 1909.

Robert Gibbings: Sweet Thames Run Softly. 1940.

L. T. C. Rolt: The Thames from Mouth to Source. 1951.

Council for the Preservation of Rural England:
            The Thames Valley from Cricklade to
            Staines, A Survey of its Existing State
            and some suggestions for its Future
            Preservation. 1929.

Concise Oxford Dictionary of English Place Names. 1964 ed.

79-423

914.22 Bergstrom, Theo
BER
The Thames

DATE